CW00346119

LOSE

WEIGHT

FOR GOOD

THE KETO DIET

FOR BEGINNERS

LOSE WEIGHT FOR GOOD: THE KETO DIET FOR BEGINNERS

COMPLETE KETOGENIC GUIDE TO FAST WEIGHT LOSS WITH LOW CARB, HIGH FAT RECIPES

Copyright © Iota Publishing Limited 2019
All rights reserved. This book or any portion thereof may not be reproduced or used in any manner whatsoever without the express written permission of the publisher.

ISBN: 9781913005184
Cover image under license from Shutterstock

Disclaimer

Except for use in any review, the reproduction or utilisation of this work in whole or in part in any form by any electronic, mechanical or other means, now known or hereafter invented, including xerography, photocopying and recording, or in any information storage or retrieval system, is forbidden without the permission of the publisher. The content of this book is available under other titles with other publishers. This book is sold subject to the condition that it shall not, by way of trade or otherwise, be lent, resold, hired out or otherwise circulated without the prior consent of the publisher in any form of binding or cover other than that in which it is published and without a similar condition including this condition being imposed on the subsequent purchaser.
Some recipes may contain nuts or traces of nuts. Those suffering from any allergies associated with nuts should avoid any recipes containing nuts or nut based oils. This information is provided and sold with the knowledge that the publisher and author do not offer any legal or other professional advice.
In the case of a need for any such expertise consult with the appropriate professional.
This book does not contain all information available on the subject, and other sources of recipes are available. Every effort has been made to make this book as accurate as possible. However, there may be typographical and or content errors. Therefore, this book should serve only as a general guide and not as the ultimate source of subject information.
This book contains information that might be dated and is intended only to educate and entertain.
The author and publisher shall have no liability or responsibility to any person or entity regarding any loss or damage incurred, or alleged to have incurred, directly or indirectly, by the information contained in this book.

CONTENTS

Dinners

Desserts 71

Drinks 87

INTRODUCTION

Based around the Keto Diet our recipes have been uniquely designed to help you manage your weight loss and maintain your goal weight, keeping you inspired and feeling energised each step of the way.

What is the Keto Diet

Unlike many new modern day diets, the Ketogenic, often shortened to 'Keto' Diet has been in existence for almost 100 years. The diet was originally designed for medical purposes by Dr Russell Wilder in 1924 as an effective method of treating epilepsy. The science upon which the diet was based centres around the process whereby the body enters the state of ketosis as a direct result of the consumption of certain foods in a controlled manner. When higher levels of fats are consumed, together with a reduction in carbohydrates, the liver plays its role in converting these natural fats into fatty acids and ketones. An increased quantity of ketones in the blood system enables ketosis. In this state the body uses fat, not carbohydrates as it's primary energy source.

When in ketosis, there are a large number of benefits to the body that can help relieve and ease the symptoms of many diseases and prevent the onset of many others. What is making the Keto Diet evermore popular is the benefit of weight loss that comes with ketosis.

Some benefits of Ketosis

- Appetite is suppressed: eating more protein and fats makes you feel fuller for longer.
- Weight loss can be quicker: studies show that cutting carbs is a faster method of shedding excess weight.
- Low carbs can be effective in reducing visceral fat in the abdominal area.
- Increased quantities of healthy fats in your diet can raise levels of HDL (High Density Lipoprotein) which is the 'good' cholesterol.
- Carbs are broken down into sugars which when then enter the blood stream. This elevates blood sugar levels and as a result the body produces more insulin to combat this. By cutting carbs you remove the need for increased insulin which if not correctly managed can lead to Type 2 Diabetes.
- A low carb diet can reduce blood pressure leading to a reduced risk of diseases such as stroke, kidney failure and heart disease.

What foods are Keto?

The Keto Diet is high-fat and low-carb, with a reasonable volume of protein. When the Keto Diet refers to fat, it is simply referring to natural fats, not processed or fast-food fats. There are a number of variations to the Keto Diet if using to treat a specific medical condition (for example epilepsy or Parkinson's), however the majority, if not all, rule out sweets, cakes and treats.

The Keto Diet is largely based around meat; mainly red meats and pork, fatty fish, such as tuna and salmon, chicken and turkey along with a good balance of eggs and dairy, such as butter, cream and unprocessed cheese. This makes the Keto Diet widely accessible, although it is encouraged that, where possible, meats and other animal products are sourced sustainably to ensure the best quality, such as grass-fed, corn-fed and free range.

Healthy oils, nuts, seeds, and healthy herbs, spices and seasonings are equally as important and can be easily added to any meal. In addition, make sure you fill up your plate with low-carb vegetables such as peppers, tomatoes, onions and largely green vegetables. Whilst fruits tend to be eliminated, the avocado is particularly favoured and beneficial in the Keto Diet due to it's high natural fatty acids..

Why eat Keto?

The Keto Diet not only helps enhance and increase the body's metabolic rate to stimulate weight loss, but it also provides several other health benefits and can be used to relieve and treat the symptoms of some illnesses and conditions when planned and managed properly.

When using the Keto Diet for the purpose of weight loss, unlike so many highly restrictive diets, the Keto Diet provides a significant range of foods that you can eat as part of your programme. This enables you to adopt the Keto Diet as a lifestyle change because it is sustainable. Many other diets cannot be followed long-term as they eliminate too many food groups, or would risk causing serious damage to the body, particularly 'fasting' diets. The Keto Diet is a healthy, controlled and balanced way to help you control and maintain your goal weight and this collection of Keto recipes is specifically designed to help manage weight loss.

How to eat Keto

Eating the 'Keto way' and adhering to a Keto Diet is relatively easy. There are different levels of Keto, depending on how strictly you wish to enforce a weight loss approach. Ratios are often referred to in the Keto Diet (for example 60-75% of calories from healthy fats, 15-30% of calories from protein and 5-10% from carbs) to ensure that your food group portions are appropriately proportioned; for example, whilst bacon and red meats can be eaten, a plate of just steak or a stack of bacon rashers is not going to provide improvements alone. Ensuring that your carbohydrate intake is kept as low as possible in conjunction with increased healthy fats and protein can aid quicker and greater weight loss. Moreover, the flexibility that the Keto Diet offers means that once you are happy with a sustained weight, you can become more liberal on your intake and ratios.

How to lose weight with Keto Diet

Essentially, the fewer carbohydrates you include with your diet, snacks and meals, the greater weight loss you should achieve.

The Keto Diet looks to exclude sugary foods, such as cake, chocolate and fruit, as well as alcohol. Whilst at first your body will miss and crave these foods, once the sugar is out of your system and you are past the 'withdrawal' stage, your body will crave foods less. Sugary foods do not keep you full for long and are designed to make your body desire more. By eating healthier alternatives including healthy fats within the Keto Diet, you are likely to feel much fuller for longer, experiencing fewer, if any, cravings and also a generally reduced hunger and appetite.

Many Keto Diet followers comment on their reduced appetite noting how they easily go longer between meals and rarely snack at all.

When following the Keto Diet your body uses fat as its energy supply. With lowered sugar levels come lowered insulin levels which enables and increases the fat burning process even more. The positive outcome is weight loss and effective weight management as part of of a properly planned and managed Keto Diet programme.

KETO DIET
BREAKFASTS

Traditional Bacon and Eggs

KETO DIET FOR BEGINNERS

Ingredients

- 1 tbsp olive oil
- 8 eggs
- 8 rashers bacon

- 8 tomatoes, halved
- 4 sprigs fresh parsley
- Salt & pepper

Method

1 Heat the oil in a frying pan and fry the bacon until crispy. Remove to a plate and set aside.

2 Fry the eggs in the same fatty pan. Add the tomato halves.

3 Season with salt and pepper to taste, and serve with a sprig of fresh parsley on each plate.

Chefs Note....
You can omit the tomatoes and parsley if you wish.

SERVES 3

Bacon and Cauliflower Fritters

**KETO DIET
FOR BEGINNERS**

Ingredients

- ½ medium cauliflower, broken into florets
- 2 tbsp double cream
- 25g/1oz butter
- Salt & pepper to taste
- 75g/3oz mozzarella cheese, grated
- 3 rashers bacon, chopped
- 1 clove garlic, peeled & crushed

- ¼ onion, chopped
- 50g/2oz leek, chopped
- 1 spring onion, chopped
- 50g/2oz Brussels sprouts, chopped
- 2 tbsp goose fat
- 25g/1oz Parmesan cheese, grated

Method

1 Tip the cauliflower into a microwaveable bowl with half the butter and the cream. Microwave on High for 4 minutes uncovered, then stir and cook again for another 4 minutes. Season with salt and pepper.

2 Blend the cauliflower mixture until creamy. Stir in the mozzarella and set aside to cool.

3 Fry the chopped bacon until it's crispy, then drain it on kitchen towel.

4 Add the remaining butter to the bacon fat in the pan. Sauté the garlic for about a minute, then add the onion and cook for about 4 or 5 minutes, until onion is translucent. Add the leek and the sprouts and cook for about 8 minutes or so, until they're tender. Add the spring onion to the pan and cook

for another minute, then remove the pan from the heat to cool.

5 Add the bacon into the onion and sprout mixture, then stir it all into the creamed cauliflower. Adjust the seasoning.

6 Melt the goose fat in a clean pan and place 3 egg rings in the pan. Sprinkle some Parmesan inside the rings. Divide half the cauliflower mixture between the rings. Sprinkle Parmesan on top. Cook on each side until a crisp crust forms.

7 When cooked, take the fritters out of the pan and keep warm while you repeat the process with the remaining Parmesan and cauliflower mixture. Serve and enjoy.

Blackberry Bake

KETO DIET
FOR BEGINNERS

Ingredients

- 5 eggs
- 15g/½oz butter, melted
- 3 tbsp coconut flour
- 1 tsp freshly grated ginger
- ¼ tsp vanilla essence
- ¼ tsp sea salt
- Zest of ½ orange
- 1 tsp fresh rosemary, finely chopped
- 50g/2oz fresh blackberries

Method

1 Preheat the oven to 175C/350F/Gas4. Grease 4 ramekins.

2 Crack the eggs into your blender. Add the butter, flour, vanilla, salt and orange zest. Blend until the mixture is smooth.

3 Sprinkle in the rosemary and pulse to mix it in.

4 Divide the mixture between the ramekins and drop a few blackberries into each.

5 Put the ramekins on a baking tray bake in the oven for 15-20 minutes until the mixture is puffed up and cooked.

6 Allow to cool for a few minutes before serving.

Chefs Note....
A delicious, unusual and filling breakfast! Feel free to substitute different berries and herbs.

Keto Granola

Ingredients

- 100g/3½oz sliced almonds
- 75g/3oz coconut flakes
- 125g/4oz walnuts, chopped
- 2 tsp cinnamon

- Stevia, or other sweetener, to taste.
- 2 tbsp coconut oil, melted

Method

1 Preheat the oven to 190C/375F/Gas5. Line a baking tray with parchment.

2 Mix all the ingredients together in a bowl. Then, scrape the mixture out onto the baking tray and spread it as evenly as possible.

3 Bake in the oven for about 10 minutes, until it begins to brown.

4 Take it out, mix it up and tip into bowls. Serve with cold unsweetened almond milk.

Chefs Note....
Store any unused granola in an airtight container for another day.

Chia and Chocolate Pudding

KETO DIET
FOR BEGINNERS

Ingredients

- 2 tbsp strong brewed coffee
- 60ml/¼ cup coconut cream
- 1 tbsp vanilla extract

- 1 tbsp granular sweetener
- 4 tbsp chia seeds
- 2 tbsp cocoa nibs

Method

1 Stir the coffee and the coconut cream together and add the vanilla and the sweetener. Stir in the chia seeds and cocoa nibs.

2 Divide the mixture between two dishes, and chill in the fridge for at least half an hour.

3 Serve with a little more coffee drizzled over the top and a sprinkling of extra cocoa nibs.

Chefs Note....
If you prefer not to drink coffee, use an organic herbal coffee substitute.

Bacon and Seafood Cream

Ingredients

- 4 rashers bacon, chopped
- 75g/3oz mushrooms, sliced
- 125g/4oz smoked salmon, sliced into strips
- 125g/4oz raw prawns, shelled
- 120ml/½ cup double cream
- Salt & pepper

Method

1 Fry the bacon in a large frying pan, stirring constantly, for about 5 minutes. Then add the mushrooms and cook for another 5 minutes, stirring frequently.

2 Stir in the smoked salmon and cook for about 2 minutes before adding the prawns. Turn up the heat and cook for a couple of minutes.

3 Pour in the cream, season with salt and pepper, then cook for another minute while the cream thickens.

4 Serve at once, with noodles or toast if you like.

Chefs Note....
If you can't tolerate dairy use coconut cream instead of double cream.

Spinach Frittata

SERVES 4

KETO DIET
FOR BEGINNERS

Ingredients

- 25g/1oz butter
- 165g/5½oz bacon, chopped
- 225g/8oz fresh spinach

- 8 eggs
- 250ml/1 cup double cream
- 165g/5½oz Cheddar cheese, grated

Method

1 Preheat the oven to 175C/350F/Gas4. Grease a baking dish.

2 Melt the butter in a frying pan and fry the bacon until crispy. Add the spinach.

3 Meanwhile, whisk together the eggs and cream then pour the mixture into the baking dish. Stir in the bacon and spinach from the frying pan and sprinkle the cheese on top.

4 Bake in the oven for 25-30 minutes. Then slice and serve.

Chefs Note....
Try also substituting sausage or chorizo for the bacon.

SERVES 4

Spiced Egg and Cheese Hash

Ingredients

- 1½ courgettes, diced
- 175g/6oz cauliflower, chopped
- ½ red pepper, deseeded & chopped
- 1 tbsp coconut oil, melted
- 1 tsp smoked paprika
- 1 tsp onion powder
- ½ tsp garlic powder
- 25g/1oz cheese, grated
- ½ medium avocado, stoned & sliced
- 3 large eggs
- 2 tsp Cajun seasoning

Method

1 Preheat the oven to 200C/400F/Gas6. Line a baking tray with foil.

2 Arrange the courgette, cauliflower and red pepper on the baking tray, and drizzle with the coconut oil. Dust on the paprika and the onion and garlic powder, and mix it up to coat evenly. Spread the vegetables back out into a single layer.

3 Bake in the oven for 10-15 minutes, until the vegetables begin to brown, then sprinkle the cheese over the top and arrange the avocado slices around the veggies. Crack the eggs into the spaces between.

4 Return to the oven and bake for about 10 minutes, until the eggs are cooked as you like them.

5 Serve sprinkled with Cajun seasoning.

Chefs Note....
If you like a really spicy breakfast, garnish with chopped jalapenos.

Breakfast Waffles

KETO DIET FOR BEGINNERS

Ingredients

- 4 eggs
- 60g/2½oz unflavoured protein powder
- 1 tsp baking powder
- 75g/3oz butter, melted
- ½ tsp sea salt

- 25g/1oz ham, finely chopped
- 25g/1oz Cheddar cheese, grated
- 1 tbsp vegetable oil
- 1 tsp dried paprika
- 2 tsp fresh basil leaves, torn

Method

1 Separate 2 of the eggs into two bowls. Whisk the protein powder, baking powder, melted butter and sea salt in with the yolks. Fold in the ham and cheese.

2 Using an electric mixer if possible, whisk the egg whites with salt until stiff. Half at a time, very gently, fold this mixture into the egg yolk mixture.

3 If you have a waffle maker, pour about 60ml/¼ cup of the batter into it at a time and cook according to the machine directions. If you don't have one, just fry them like pancakes.

4 Meanwhile, heat the oil or butter in a separate pan, and fry the remaining eggs.

5 When the waffles are ready, divide them between 2 plates, and top each with a fried egg. Serve garnished with paprika and torn fresh basil leaves.

Chefs Note....
Feel free to vary the cheese and herbs, and fry the eggs in butter if you prefer.

Cauliflower Hash Browns

Ingredients

- ½ large cauliflower, riced
- 1 egg, beaten
- ¼ onion, finely chopped
- ¼ green pepper, finely chopped

- ¼ red pepper, finely chopped
- Salt & pepper
- ½ tbsp olive oil
- 50g/2oz cheese, grated

Method

1 In a bowl, mix together the cauliflower, egg, onion and peppers. Season with salt and pepper.

2 Heat the oil in small frying pan and spoon in half the cauliflower mixture. Flatten down and shape it into a square or circle. Cook for about 5 minutes, until the bottom is golden brown and crisp. Then turn it over and sprinkle on half the cheese.

3 Cook for another 3-4 minutes until the cheese is melted. Then, remove from the pan and cook the rest of the cauliflower mixture in the same way, topping with the remaining cheese to serve.

Chefs Note....
Make cauliflower rice by pulsing it in your food processor until it resembles couscous.

Seed and Nut Porridge

KETO DIET
FOR BEGINNERS

Ingredients

- 250ml/1 cup almond milk
- 60g/2½oz shelled hemp seeds, + 1 tbsp
- 2 tbsp flax seeds, ground
- 1 tbsp chia seeds
- Liquid sweetener, to taste

- ¾ tsp vanilla extract
- ½ tsp ground cinnamon
- 25g/1oz ground almonds
- 3 Brazil nuts, chopped

Method

1 Pour the almond milk into a pan. Stir in 60g/2½oz hemp seeds, the flax seeds, chia seeds, sweetener, vanilla and cinnamon.

2 Bring gently to the boil, then stir and simmer for a couple more minutes.

3 Take the pan off the heat and stir in the crushed almonds.

4 Turn the porridge out into a bowl. Place the Brazil nuts on top and scatter with the remaining hemp seeds. Serve at once.

Chefs Note....
Use a different non-dairy milk if you prefer, e.g. coconut or soy.

Corned Beef Hash

KETO DIET
FOR BEGINNERS

Ingredients

- 1 tbsp olive oil
- 1 small onion, chopped
- 450g/1lb radishes, roughly chopped
- 2 cloves garlic, peeled & crushed

- 120ml/½ cup beef stock
- 225g/8oz corned beef, chopped
- Salt & pepper

Method

1 Heat the oil in a pan and sauté the onions for 3-4 minutes until translucent.

2 Add the radishes and cook for another 5 minutes. Stir in the garlic and cook for a minute, then mix in the stock.

3 Cover and cook for around 5 minutes, until the radishes are tender and the liquid is absorbed.

4 Stir in the corned beef.

5 Season with salt and pepper to taste, and serve.

Chefs Note....
Cooked radishes are used here as a potato substitute. Feel free to add any vegetables you have – delicious with cabbage or kale!

Mediterranean Scrambled Egg

KETO DIET
FOR BEGINNERS

Ingredients

- 2 tbsp olive oil
- 75g/3oz halloumi cheese, cubed
- 2 spring onions, chopped
- 4 rashers bacon, chopped

- 4 eggs
- 6 tbsp fresh parsley, chopped
- Salt & pepper
- 6 tbsp olives, pitted

Method

1 Heat the olive oil in a frying pan, and fry the halloumi with the spring onions and bacon until the bacon is crisp.

2 Meanwhile, whisk together the eggs and parsley, and season with salt and pepper.

3 Pour the egg mixture over the bacon and cheese in the frying pan. Reduce the heat, and stir in the olives.

4 Cook, stirring, for a couple of minutes, until the egg is firmed up to your liking.

5 Serve alone, or with salad.

Chefs Note....
Makes a delicious and filling breakfast or lunch.

Smoked Salmon Balls

KETO DIET
FOR BEGINNERS

Ingredients

- 2 large eggs, hard boiled & shelled, + 1 egg yolk
- 125g/4oz smoked salmon, finely chopped
- Knob of butter, + 25g/1oz
- 2 tbsp fresh chives, chopped
- Salt & pepper
- ¼ tsp Dijon mustard
- 2 tsp fresh lemon juice

Method

1 Melt a knob of butter in a pan and fry about half the chopped salmon until the pieces are crisp. Remove from the heat and when cooled mix them with the chives. Set aside.

2 Mash the hard-boiled eggs in a bowl with a fork.

3 Bring a pan of water to a simmer, and melt 25g/1oz butter in the microwave for about 30 seconds.

4 In a bowl that will fit over the pan of simmering water, whisk the egg yolk with the lemon juice, mustard and a pinch of salt. Fit the bowl over the simmering pan of water, making sure the water doesn't quite reach the bottom of the bowl.

5 Whisk the egg mixture until it starts to thicken, then gradually pour in the melted butter, still whisking. Cook, stirring until the sauce thickens fully. Take it off the heat and set aside to cool to room temperature.

6 In a clean bowl, mix together the remaining, uncooked salmon, the cooled sauce, half the chives, and the mashed boiled eggs, until they're thoroughly combined.

7 Divide the mixture into four even pieces and roll each into balls. Roll the balls in the chives and crispy salmon mixture to coat. Then serve and enjoy!

Apple and Cheese Crepes

Ingredients

- 125g/4oz cream cheese
- 4 eggs
- ½ tsp baking soda
- ¼ tsp salt
- Knob of butter, + 15g/½oz

- 50g/2oz pecan nuts, chopped
- ¼ tsp ground cinnamon
- 1 small, sweet apple, cored & finely sliced
- 125g/4oz Brie cheese, finely sliced
- Fresh mint leaves, to garnish

Method

1 Using a blender, blend together the cream cheese, eggs, baking soda and salt, until you have a smooth batter.

2 Melt a knob of butter in a frying pan. Ladle a little batter into the pan and swirl into a thin layer. Cook for 2 or 3 minutes, until the top looks dry, then carefully turn it and cook the other side for a few seconds.

3 Remove from the pan and keep warm while you cook the rest of the batter into about 12 crepes.

4 In a small pan, melt the remaining butter and fry the pecans until they're fragrant. Sprinkle them with

the cinnamon and stir to coat. Cool them on a plate.

5 Arrange the slices of apple and cheese on the crepes and sprinkle some toasted pecans over the top. Serve garnished with mint.

Chefs Note....
Alternatively, use more batter at a time and make fewer, thicker pancakes.

KETO DIET
LUNCHES

LOSE
WEIGHT
FOR GOOD
THE KETO DIET
FOR BEGINNERS

Cheesy 'Wrap'

KETO DIET
FOR BEGINNERS

Ingredients

- Non-stick cooking spray
- 200g/7oz Cheddar cheese
- 225g/8oz minced beef, cooked

- 50g/2oz tomatoes, chopped
- ½ avocado, stoned & chopped
- Dash Tabasco sauce, to taste

Method

1 Preheat the oven to 200C/400F/Gas6.

2 Line a small baking tray with parchment, leaving flaps on either side for lifting. Spray the parchment with non-stick oil, especially at the edges.

3 Scatter the cheese all over the base of the tray in one complete layer. (Use more cheese if necessary). Bake it in the oven for about 15 minutes, or until the cheese bubbles and browns on the top and you can slide a spatula under it to remove it.

4 When it's ready, spoon the mince over it and cook for another 10 minutes until it's piping hot.

5 Meanwhile, in a bowl, mix together the tomatoes, avocado and Tabasco. When the cheese wrap is out of the oven, spoon on the tomato mixture in a single layer.

6 Cut it into 4 slices and roll each slice up into a wrap. Serve and enjoy.

Chefs Note....
You can fill the wrap with anything you like. It's a great way to use up leftovers! Try also with Bolognese sauce, or a dash of Sriracha.

SERVES 2

Cauliflower Pizza

KETO DIET
FOR BEGINNERS

Ingredients

- ½ cauliflower, riced
- 75g/3oz almond flour
- 1 tsp garlic powder
- 1 tsp onion powder
- 1 tsp dried oregano

- 2 tsp olive oil
- 1 egg, beaten
- 1 small tomato sliced
- 50g/2oz pepperoni
- 50g/2oz rocket

Method

1 Preheat the oven to 180C/350F/Gas4. Line a baking tray with parchment.

2 Microwave the cauliflower rice on High for about 2 minutes, then tip it onto a muslin square or clean, fine tea towel. When the rice is cool enough to handle, wrap it up in the muslin and squeeze out all the liquid you can.

3 Tip the cauliflower into a bowl and mix it with the almond flour, garlic powder, onion powder, dried oregano, olive oil, and egg to form a dough.

4 Turn the dough out onto the baking tray and shape it into a thin round pizza base.

5 Bake in the oven for 10 minutes.

6 Take it out and arrange the tomato and pepperoni on the base, then return it to the oven and bake for another 10 minutes.

7 Drizzle the pizza with a little olive oil and spread the rocket over the top.

8 Slice and serve immediately.

Chefs Note....
To make cauliflower 'rice', whizz the cauliflower in a food processor.

Tuna and Egg Salad

KETO DIET
FOR BEGINNERS

Ingredients

- 125g/4oz tinned tuna in olive oil, drained
- 2 stalks celery, chopped
- ½ red onion, peeled & chopped
- 125g/4oz mayonnaise
- 1 tsp Dijon mustard
- 2 tbsp capers
- ½ lemon, juice and zest
- Salt & pepper
- 2 tsp white vinegar
- 4 eggs
- 50g/2oz lettuce
- 50g/2oz cherry tomatoes, halved
- 2 tbsp extra virgin olive oil

Method

1 In a bowl, combine the tuna with the celery, onion, mayonnaise, mustard, capers, and the lemon juice and zest. Season the salad with salt and pepper to taste.

2 Fill a pan with water and bring it to a gentle boil. Add the vinegar and a teaspoon of salt. Stir the water to create a swirl and crack in the eggs, one at a time. Cook for 2-4 minutes, according to your preference, then remove the eggs with a slotted spoon.

3 Divide the lettuce and tomato halves between 2 plates. Serve the tuna salad and the eggs on top. Drizzle generously with olive oil, and enjoy.

Chefs Note....
If you make the tuna salad in advance and store it in the fridge, this is a quick and easy lunch – and it's filling too!

Stuffed Lettuce Leaves

KETO DIET
FOR BEGINNERS

Ingredients

- 2 tbsp butter
- ½ red pepper, deseeded & chopped
- ½ green pepper, deseeded & chopped
- 4 stalks celery, finely chopped
- 900g/2lb boneless, skinless chicken thighs, chopped

- 2 tsp onion powder
- 1 tsp garlic powder
- Salt & pepper
- 50g/2oz blue cheese, crumbled
- 2 spring onions, chopped
- 8 crisp leaves from a round lettuce

Method

1 Melt the butter in a large frying pan and sauté the peppers and celery for about 5 minutes until they begin to soften.

2 Stir in the chicken, onion powder, and garlic powder, and season with salt and pepper. Cook for another 4 or 5 minutes, until the chicken is cooked through.

3 Remove the pan from heat and stir in the blue cheese and spring onions.

4 Fill the lettuce leaves with the chicken mixture and serve hot or cold.

Chefs Note....
These make an excellent packed lunch. If you have time, feel free to substitute chopped fresh onion and garlic for the time-saving powders.

Spicy Broccoli Salad

Ingredients

- 1½ heads broccoli, roughly chopped
- ½ red pepper, deseeded & chopped
- 250g/9oz mayonnaise
- 50g/2oz Cheddar cheese
- 2 tbsp sunflower seeds

- 6 rashers bacon, fried & crumbled
- ½ tbsp cider vinegar
- 1 tsp sriracha sauce
- Salt & pepper to taste

Method

1 Combine all the ingredients in a bowl.

2 Stir them together well, then tip them out into an airtight container.

3 Chill in the fridge for at least 2 hours to let the flavours infuse.

4 Serve.

Chefs Note....
Sriracha sauce is a lovely spicy condiment available in most larger supermarkets.

Smoked Salmon and Cream Cheese Rolls

KETO DIET
FOR BEGINNERS

Ingredients

- 4 large slices of ham
- 2 tbsp cream cheese
- ½ cucumber, finely sliced lengthwise

- 100g/3½oz smoked salmon
- Mixed salad leaves, to serve

Method

1 Set out the slices of ham on a board or worktop.

2 Spread the cream cheese on each slice then cover with slices of smoked salmon. Add the cucumber slices on top.

3 Roll the ham up, and serve 2 each with lots of green salad.

Chefs Note....
You can use coconut cream instead of cream cheese if you wish to avoid dairy produce.

Warm Goat's Cheese Salad

KETO DIET FOR BEGINNERS

Ingredients

- 2 tbsp poppy seeds
- 2 tbsp sesame seeds
- 1 tsp dried onion
- 1 tsp garlic granules
- 125g/4oz goat's cheese, thickly sliced
- Cooking spray

- 1 red pepper, deseeded and roughly chopped
- 40g/1½oz mushrooms, sliced
- 75g/3oz rocket
- 1 tbsp extra virgin olive oil

Method

1 In a small bowl, mix together the poppy seeds, sesame seeds, dried onion and garlic granules.

2 Coat each slice of goat's cheese in the mixture, and set it aside in the fridge.

3 Divide the rocket between 2 plates or bowls.

4 Spray a frying pan with non-stick oil and heat. Cook the peppers and mushrooms until the pepper softens and they're slightly charred. Arrange them on top of the plates of rocket.

5 Fry the coated goat cheese in the same pan, for about 30 seconds on each side.

6 Divide the slices between the salad plates, then drizzle both with the olive oil.

7 Serve while the cheese and vegetables are still warm.

Chefs Note....
This makes a tasty, crunchy and satisfying lunch.

Mushroom Omelette

KETO DIET
FOR BEGINNERS

Ingredients

- 3 eggs
- Salt & pepper
- 25g/1oz butter

- 25g/1oz Cheddar cheese, grated
- 1/4 onion, peeled & chopped
- 3 mushrooms, sliced

Method

1 Whisk the eggs in a bowl with a little salt and pepper.

2 Melt the butter in a frying pan, then pour in the eggs.

3 Once the omelette is firm underneath but still uncooked on top, scatter on the cheese, onion and mushroom.

4 Fold the omelette over with a spatula, and then fold it over in half.

5 When it's golden brown on the bottom, serve and enjoy with salad.

Chefs Note....

Feel free to use any cheese you prefer, and add whatever keto-friendly vegetables you have to hand, e.g. red or green pepper, spinach or broccoli.

Cauliflower Curry

KETO DIET
FOR BEGINNERS

Ingredients

- 350g/12oz Greek yogurt
- 1 tsp Cayenne pepper
- 1 tsp smoked paprika
- 2 tbsp curry powder
- 1 lime, juiced, ½ zested
- Salt & pepper
- 1 cauliflower

- 75g/3oz pine nuts
- 1 clove garlic, peeled
- 15g/½oz sun-dried tomatoes in oil, drained
- 25g/1oz feta cheese, crumbled
- 1 tbsp fresh coriander, chopped
- 3 tbsp olive oil

Method

1 Preheat the oven to 190C/375F/Gas5. Line a baking tray with parchment.

2 Pour the yogurt into a bowl and mix in the Cayenne pepper, paprika, curry powder and the lime juice and zest. Season to taste.

3 Rub this mixture all over the cauliflower head, then place it on the baking tray and bake it the oven for about 45 minutes until it's golden and crispy.

4 Place it in a serving dish and set aside.

5 Tip half the pine nuts, the garlic and the sun-dried tomatoes into your food processor and pulse into a chunky mixture.

6 Scrape it out into a small bowl and stir in the rest of the pine nuts, the feta, coriander and olive oil.

7 Drizzle over the roasted cauliflower and break it all down into a delicious chunky curry. Serve warm.

Chefs Note....
Delicious on its own for lunch or as a side dish with your main meal.

Courgette Noodles with Garlic Butter

KETO DIET FOR BEGINNERS

Ingredients

- 40g/1½oz butter
- 1 tbsp garlic infused olive oil
- 2 cloves garlic, peeled & crushed
- ¼ red pepper, finely chopped
- 1 tsp dried chilli flakes

- 2 courgettes, cut lengthwise into strips with a potato peeler
- 1 tbsp fresh basil, chopped
- 50g/2oz Parmesan cheese, grated
- Salt & pepper

Method

1 Melt the butter and garlic infused oil in a pan. Sauté the garlic, red pepper and chilli flakes together for 1 minute, then stir in the courgette. Cook for another minute, then remove from the heat.

2 Quickly stir in the basil and half the Parmesan.

3 Empty the mixture out into a bowl and sprinkle with the remaining Parmesan.

4 Serve immediately.

Chefs Note....
The courgettes would ideally be spiralized. If you don't have a spiralizer use a potatoes peeler to cut into thin strips.

Tuna with Roasted Vegetables

KETO DIET
FOR BEGINNERS

Ingredients

- 1 cauliflower, broken into florets
- 1 head broccoli, broken into florets
- 2 tbsp olive oil
- ½ lemon, juiced

- Salt & pepper
- 4 x 160g/5oz tins tuna in oil
- 3 tbsp fresh parsley, chopped

Method

1 Preheat the oven to 200C/400F/Gas6.

2 Arrange the cauliflower and broccoli on a baking tray and drizzle them with 1 tbsp olive oil and half the lemon juice.

3 Sprinkle with a little salt. Mix it all up to coat the vegetables thoroughly then spread the out in a single layer if you can.

4 Roast in the oven for about 20 minutes, or until everything is softened and brown at the edges.

5 Tip them out into a large bowl and mix in the parsley, and the remaining olive oil and lemon juice. Adjust the seasoning.

6 Divide the vegetables between 4 bowls and top with a flaked can of tuna. Serve warm.

Chefs Note....
If you don't need it all at once, store leftovers in the fridge for later. Feel free to substitute any meat or oily fish for the tuna.

Pesto, Cheese & Tomato Filled Flatbread

KETO DIET FOR BEGINNERS

Ingredients

- Cooking spray
- 125g/4oz almond flour
- 3 tbsp mozzarella liquid
- 1 large egg
- 25g/1oz Parmesan cheese, grated

- 1 tsp garlic powder
- 2 tbsp pesto
- 4 fresh basil leaves
- 15g/½oz Mozzarella, sliced
- 4 cherry tomatoes

Method

1 Heat the oven to 190C/375°F/Gas5. Line a baking tray with parchment and spray it with non-stick oil.

2 In a bowl, mix the almond flour with the liquid from the mozzarella packet. Stir in the egg, Parmesan cheese and garlic powder to form a dough ball.

3 Roll the dough into a ball and place on the baking tray. Press it down to make a circle, about 1cm thick all over.

4 Spread pesto evenly over the dough circle, except the edge. Arrange the mozzarella slices, basil leaves, and tomatoes in layers on top of the pesto.

5 Fold up the edges of the dough over the filling. Use the parchment to help.

6 Bake in the oven for 20-25 minutes, until the crust is golden brown and the cheese is melted.

7 Cut into 3 and serve.

Chefs Note....
Feel free to vary the fillings inside your cheesy flatbread.

Mince with Cabbage and Cheese

Ingredients

- 165g/5½oz butter
- 750g/1lb11oz white cabbage, finely shredded
- 1 tsp onion granules
- 2 tsp dried thyme
- 1 tbsp white wine vinegar

- Salt & pepper
- 550g/1¼ lbs minced beef
- 165g/5½oz blue cheese
- 250ml/1 cup double cream
- 8 tbsp fresh parsley, chopped

Method

1 Melt half the butter in a large frying pan and sauté the cabbage until it softens.

2 Stir in the onion granules, thyme and vinegar.

3 Cook for a minute or two longer, then tip it out into a bowl. Set aside.

4 In the same pan, melt the remaining butter. Brown the mince and cook until most of the juices have evaporated.

5 Reduce the heat, then stir in the cheese until it's melted. Pour in the cream and simmer, stirring, for a few more minutes.

6 Tip the cabbage back into the pan, and stir it through.

7 Cook for a few minutes until everything is piping hot. Adjust the seasoning, and serve sprinkled with fresh parsley.

Chefs Note....
This quick and easy recipe makes a moreish lunch or dinner. Substitute cheddar cheese for blue cheese if you prefer.

Egg Stuffed Avocado

Ingredients

- 3 avocados, halved & stoned
- 6 eggs
- 1 tsp garlic granules
- Salt & pepper
- 25g/1oz Parmesan cheese, grated

Method

1 Preheat the oven to 175C/350F/Gas4.

2 Scoop out about a third of the flesh from each avocado half, and place them on a baking tray or muffin tin, cut sides up. Sprinkle each with garlic powder, salt and pepper.

3 Crack an egg into each half and scatter the cheese over the top.

4 Bake in the oven for 10-15 minutes, until the egg is cooked to your liking.

5 Serve and enjoy!

Chefs Note....
A simple and satisfying lunch to keep you going all afternoon. Also makes a great breakfast.

Caesar Salad

Ingredients

- 1 ripe avocado, peeled, stoned & sliced
- 125g/4oz salad leaves
- 2 chicken breasts, grilled & sliced

- 4 rashers bacon, crumbled
- 4 tbsp Caesar salad dressing

Method

1 Divide the avocado, leaves, chicken and bacon between two bowls and mix the ingredients together.

2 Spoon half the salad dressing on top of each bowl, and serve.

Chefs Note....
Really quick to prepare if you've cooked the chicken and bacon in advance. Makes a great packed lunch, too, although you shouldn't mix the ingredients until you're ready to eat.

Salmon Curry

KETO DIET
FOR BEGINNERS

Ingredients

- 2 tbsp coconut oil
- ½ onion, peeled & finely chopped
- 1 clove garlic, peeled & crushed
- 200g/7oz green beans, chopped
- 1½ tbsp curry powder

- 400ml/14floz can coconut milk, refrigerated
- 500ml/2 cups fish or vegetable stock
- 450g/1lb salmon fillets, chopped
- Salt & pepper, to taste
- 2 tbsp fresh basil, to garnish

Method

1 Melt the coconut oil in a pan and sauté the onion for about 4 minutes, until translucent.

2 Stir in the garlic and green beans and cook for a few minutes more. Pour in the stock and bring to the boil, stirring occasionally.

3 Reduce the heat and gently stir in the curry powder and the salmon.

4 Scoop the cream off the top of the refrigerated can of coconut milk and stir it into the curry. Simmer for about 4 minutes, until the salmon is cooked.

5 Season to taste and serve garnished with basil leaves.

Chefs Note....
Salmon is a naturally oily fish, high in omega 3.

Egg and Cheese Salad

KETO DIET
FOR BEGINNERS

Ingredients

- 2 tbsp soured cream
- 2 tbsp mayonnaise
- ½ tsp dried garlic granules
- ½ tsp dried onion granules
- 1 tsp dried parsley
- 1 tbsp milk

- 200g/7oz lettuce, shredded
- 3 hard-boiled eggs, sliced
- 125g/4oz Cheddar cheese, cubed
- 100g/3½oz cherry tomatoes, halved
- 100g/3½oz cucumber
- 1 tbsp Dijon mustard

Method

1 In a small bowl, mix together the soured cream, mayonnaise, and dried garlic, onion and parsley. Stir in the milk.

2 Line the bottom of a serving bowl with lettuce, then add the egg, cheese, tomatoes and cucumber. Drop the mustard in the centre.

3 Drizzle the creamy dressing over the top and mix everything up to coat the salad.

Chefs Note....
The rich dressing on top of the cheese, makes this salad high in fat – great for a tasty, crunchy, meat-free lunch.

Tomato, Basil and Mozzarella Omelette

KETO DIET
FOR BEGINNERS

Ingredients

- 6 eggs, beaten
- Salt & pepper
- 1 tbsp fresh basil, chopped

- 2 tbsp olive oil
- 100g/3½oz cherry tomatoes, halved
- 165g/5½oz mozzarella cheese, shredded

Method

1 Whisk the eggs in a bowl with the salt and pepper and basil.

2 Heat the oil in a frying pan, and fry the tomatoes for a minute or two. Then pour the egg on top. When the egg begins to firm, scatter the mozzarella cheese evenly over the omelette. Lower the heat and leave it to set.

3 Serve as soon as the omelette is ready.

Chefs Note....
This omelette is easy, nourishing and high in fat.

Cheese Toastie

SERVES 1

KETO DIET FOR BEGINNERS

Ingredients

- 2 eggs
- 2 tbsp water
- 25g/1oz butter, melted
- 2 tbsp coconut flour
- ½ tsp baking powder

- 1 tsp dried oregano
- ½ tsp salt
- ½ tsp black pepper
- Cheese, sliced

Method

1 Whisk the eggs with the water. Stir in half the melted butter.

2 Mix in the coconut flour, baking powder, oregano and seasoning to make a smooth dough.

3 Turn the dough out into a square microwavable dish and spread it evenly. Cook in the microwave for about 2 minutes until cooked and firm.

4 Remove the bread from the dish and cut it in half to make 2 slices.

5 Heat the remaining butter in a frying pan and fry one slice of bread until golden brown.

6 Place the other slice in the pan and arrange the cheese on top. Close the sandwich with the first slice and cook until the cheese melts.

Chefs Note....
Feel free to add any keto-friendly filling you like with the cheese.

Goat's Cheese Balls

Ingredients

- 125g/4oz goat cheese
- 25g/1oz sun dried tomatoes, chopped
- 50g/2oz pistachio nuts, chopped
- Salt to taste

Method

1 Cut your goat cheese into 8 equal slices.

2 Place the chopped sundried tomatoes on top of each slice, then roll together into 8 balls.

3 Mix the chopped pistachios with a little salt and roll each cheese ball in the nuts to coat.

4 Serve.

Chefs Note....
A speedy lunch to eat on the go, or serve on plates with green salad and tomatoes.

KETO DIET

DINNERS

LOSE
WEIGHT
FOR GOOD
THE KETO DIET
FOR BEGINNERS

Goulash

KETO DIET
FOR BEGINNERS

Ingredients

- 4 tbsp olive oil
- ½ onion, peeled & chopped
- 2 cloves garlic, peeled & chopped
- 450b/1lb stewing steak, chopped into bite-size pieces
- 50g/2oz mushrooms, chopped
- ½ red pepper, deseeded & chopped

- ½ green pepper, deseeded & chopped
- 120ml/½ cup beef stock
- 1 bay leaf
- 1 tbsp smoked paprika
- 75g/3oz tomatoes, finely chopped
- Salt & pepper, to taste

Method

1 Heat the oil in a large pan, and sauté the onion and garlic for about 5 minutes, until the onion is translucent, then tip in the beef and brown it.

2 Stir in the mushroom and peppers and cook for another 5 minutes. Pour in the stock, then add the bay leaf, and stir in the paprika and tomato.

3 Lower the heat, cover and simmer gently for an hour, stirring occasionally.

4 When the meat is tender and the sauce thick enough, season to taste and remove the bay leaf.

5 Serve with cauliflower rice, scattered with chopped parsley.

Chefs Note....
For a creamier sauce, stir in 2 tablespoons of double cream before you serve.

50

Chicken Curry

Ingredients

- 2 tbsp coconut oil
- 8 boneless, skinless chicken thighs, chopped
- 1 onion, peeled & roughly chopped
- 3 courgettes, roughly chopped
- 2 cloves garlic, peeled & crushed

- 1 tbsp curry powder
- ½ tsp paprika
- 2 tsp salt
- 2 x 400ml/14floz cans coconut milk
- 200g/7oz tomatoes, chopped
- Coriander, chopped, to garnish

Method

1 Heat the coconut oil in a large pan, and fry the chicken pieces until browned. Transfer the chicken to a plate and set aside.

2 Add the onion and courgette to the remaining oil in the same pan and sauté for about 5 minutes. Stir in the garlic, curry powder, paprika, and salt.

3 Return the chicken to the pan and pour in the coconut milk.

4 Bring to the boil, then lower the heat, cover and simmer for about half an hour, until the chicken is tender.

5 Stir in the tomatoes and cook for a further 5 minutes.

6 Ladle into bowls and scatter with fresh coriander.

Chefs Note....
Serve with cooked, riced cauliflower if you wish.

Meatball Casserole

SERVES 4

KETO DIET
FOR BEGINNERS

Ingredients

- 450g/1lb steak mince
- 1 tsp dried oregano
- 1 tsp dried thyme
- Salt & pepper
- 1 tbsp olive oil
- 2 x 400g/14oz tinned chopped tomatoes

- 1 small red onion, peeled & chopped
- 2 cloves garlic, peeled & crushed
- 1 tbsp tomato puree
- 50g/2oz mozzarella cheese, grated
- Handful fresh basil, chopped

Method

1 Preheat the oven to 190C/375F/Gas5.

2 In a bowl mix together the mince, oregano and thyme. Season well with salt and pepper. With your hands, shape 16 meatballs from the mince mixture.

3 Heat the oil in pan, and fry the meatballs for about 5 minutes, until they're evenly browned. With a slotted spoon, transfer the meatballs to a bowl.

4 Leaving about a tablespoon of the cooking juices still in the pan, pour in the can of tomatoes, then stir in the onion, garlic and tomato puree.

5 Breakdown the tomatoes into small chunks and mix the sauce well. Simmer for about 10 minutes, until the sauce thickens.

6 Place the meatballs in a casserole dish and pour the tomato sauce over them. Scatter the mozzarella over the top of the casserole.

7 Cover and bake in the oven for 20 minutes, then remove the cover and bake for another 5 minutes to brown the cheese.

8 Sprinkle the fresh basil over the top, and serve with salad or leafy greens.

Chefs Note....
Use grated Cheddar or Parmesan if you prefer.

Slow Cooker Pulled Pork Wraps

Ingredients

- 900g/2lb pork shoulder
- 1 tbsp salt
- 1 tsp pepper
- 1 tsp ground cinnamon
- 2 tsp garlic granules
- 1 tsp ground cumin
- 250ml/1 cup chicken stock
- 2 tbsp cider vinegar

- 1 onion, peeled & chopped
- 4 cloves garlic, peeled & chopped
- 8 keto-friendly wraps
- 8 tbsp guacamole
- 100g/3½oz cheese, grated
- 250ml/1cup sour cream
- Handful fresh coriander leaves, chopped

Method

1 Score the pork with a knife. In a small bowl combine the salt, pepper, cinnamon, and rub the mixture all over the meat, especially the scored crevices.

2 Pour the chicken stock and cider vinegar into your slow cooker. Add the onion and garlic.

3 Place the pork shoulder in the slow cooker, cover and cook on Low for 8-10 hours.

4 Remove the pork to a plate or board and shred it with 2 forks. Sieve the liquid from the slow cooker, retaining the onion and garlic. Mix the onion and garlic in with the pulled pork, and adjust the seasoning.

5 Spread out the wraps on your worktop. Layer on the pulled pork, guacamole and cheese. Add a dollop of soured cream to each, and a sprinkling of coriander.

6 Serve and enjoy with fresh tomatoes and green salad.

Chefs Note....
Slow cooking the meat is ideal for pulled pork, since it shreds easily, but you could oven or pot roast it instead.

Tropical Steak

Ingredients

- 120ml/½ cup coconut oil, melted
- Zest and juice of 1 lime
- 3 cloves garlic, peeled & crushed
- 1 tsp freshly grated ginger

- 1 tsp dried chilli flakes
- Salt & pepper
- 4 sirloin steaks, each weighing approx. 225g/8oz

Method

1 In a large bowl, mix together the coconut oil, lime juice and zest, garlic, ginger and chilli flakes. Season well with salt and pepper.

2 Add the steaks, turning to coat, and marinate them for at least 20 minutes.

3 Heat a frying pan over high heat and sear the steaks on both sides. Cook in batches, if necessary, and spoon any leftover marinade over the steaks as they cook.

4 Cook the steaks as you like them, then remove them from the pan and allow to rest for a few minutes

5 Serve with wilted spinach or other keto-friendly vegetable.

Chefs Note....
A particularly delicious way to enjoy tender steak.

Chicken Kiev

KETO DIET
FOR BEGINNERS

Ingredients

- 2 chicken breasts
- 4 cloves garlic, peeled & crushed
- 4 tbsp ghee
- 1 egg

- 50g/2oz coconut flour
- 2 tbsp garlic granules
- 1 tsp salt

Method

1 Preheat the oven to 220C/425F/Gas7.

2 Pound the chicken breasts until they're thin enough to roll. Divide the crushed garlic and ghee between each breast, then roll them up with the mixture inside.

3 Whisk the egg in a bowl. In another bowl, combine the coconut flour, garlic granules and salt.

4 Dip the rolled chicken into the egg and then into the coconut flour mix to coat. Place them on a baking tray and bake them in the oven for about 35 minutes, until the chicken is cooked and the coating crispy.

5 Serve hot with green vegetables.

Chefs Note....
Alternatively, you can dig out a small hole in the chicken breasts and stuff the ghee and garlic in there.

Cauliflower Cheese

KETO DIET
FOR BEGINNERS

Ingredients

- 1 cauliflower, broken into florets
- 120ml/½ cup kefir
- 125g/4oz cottage cheese, pureed
- 1 tsp Dijon mustard

- 150g/5oz Cheddar cheese, + extra to garnish
- Salt & pepper
- Pinch garlic granules

Method

1 Preheat the oven to 190C/375F/Gas5. Grease a baking dish with butter or ghee.

2 Cook the cauliflower in boiling water for about 5 minutes and until slightly tender. Drain it and dry with kitchen towel. Arrange the florets in the greased dish.

3 In a pan, heat the kefir, cottage cheese, and mustard, stirring until smooth. Stir in the Cheddar and garlic granules and season well with salt and pepper. Cook, stirring, until the cheese just starts to melt.

4 Pour the cheese mixture over the cauliflower in

the baking dish and stir them together. Scatter the extra cheese over the top and bake in the oven for 10-15 minutes.

5 Serve as a main dish with a crunchy salad on the side, or as an accompaniment to meat.

Chefs Note....
This is almost like macaroni and cheese! Vary the flavours and textures by using goat's and ewe's cheese as well as cow's.

Slow Cooked Chicken and Mushroom Stew

SERVES 4

KETO DIET FOR BEGINNERS

Ingredients

- 675g/1½lb button mushrooms
- 250ml/1 cup chicken stock
- 450g/1lb chicken breast, chopped into bite-sized pieces
- ½ tsp dried basil
- ½ tsp dried oregano
- ¼ tsp dried thyme

- 2 bay leaves
- Salt & pepper
- 25g/1oz butter
- 60ml/¼ cup double cream
- 8 rashers bacon, fried and crumbled
- 3 tbsp fresh parsley, chopped

Method

1 Tip the mushrooms into your slow cooker.

2 Pour in the chicken stock, then stir in the chicken, basil, oregano, thyme, garlic, and bay leaves. Season with salt and pepper.

3 Cover and cook on Low for 4-5 hours or on High for 2-3.

4 Stir in the butter and cream, remove the bay leaves and adjust the seasoning.

5 Serve in bowls sprinkled with the crumbled bacon and chopped parsley.

Chefs Note....
If you don't have a slow cooker, use a large, covered pan, and cook on low heat for an hour.

Shepherd's Pie

KETO DIET
FOR BEGINNERS

Ingredients

- 4 tbsp olive oil
- 450g/1lb minced lamb
- ½ onion, peeled & chopped
- 3 cloves garlic, peeled & crushed
- 1 stalk celery, chopped
- 200g/7oz tomatoes, chopped

- 675g/1½lb riced cauliflower, cooked
- 250ml/1 cup double cream
- 100g/3½oz Cheddar cheese, grated
- 25g/1oz Parmesan cheese, grated
- 1 tsp dried thyme

Method

1 Preheat the oven to 175C/350F/Gas4.

2 Heat the oil in a large frying pan, and brown the mince with the onion, garlic and celery. Remove from the heat and stir in the tomatoes.

3 Pour it all into a casserole dish.

4 In a blender or food processor, blend together the cauliflower, cream, cheese and thyme until it resembles mashed potato. Spread the mixture over the mince in the casserole dish.

5 Bake in the oven for 35-40 minutes.

6 Allow to cool for a minute or two, then slice and serve.

Chefs Note....
To make cooked cauliflower 'rice' whizz the cauliflower in a food processor then microwave on High for about 2 minutes.

Slow-Cooked Beef Stew

KETO DIET FOR BEGINNERS

Ingredients

- 675g/1½lb stewing steak
- 2 x 400g/14oz tinned chopped tomatoes
- 1 tbsp dried chili flakes
- 250ml/1 cup beef stock

- 1 tsp Tabasco sauce
- 1 tbsp Worcestershire sauce
- Salt & pepper

Method

1 Mix all the ingredients together in your slow cooker.

2 Cover and cook on Low for 8-10 hours, or on High for 6 hours.

3 Stir, and using a fork, break the meat apart into bite-sized chunks, or shred it if you prefer.

4 Adjust the seasoning, re-cover and cook on Low for another hour.

5 Serve with green leafy vegetables or green beans.

Chefs Note....
Use more chilli flakes and Tabasco sauce if you like more heat.

Lemon Chicken

KETO DIET
FOR BEGINNERS

Ingredients

- 40g/1½oz pistachios, finely chopped
- 3 tbsp toasted sesame seeds
- 1 tbsp dried parsley
- Zest of 1 lemon, + 2 lemons, thickly sliced
- 1 tsp onion powder
- 1 tsp chilli powder

- ½ tsp ground cumin
- ½ tsp ground coriander
- Salt & pepper
- 4 boneless, skinless chicken breasts, each weighing approx. 225g/8oz
- 3 tbsp olive oil

Method

1 Preheat the oven to 175C/350F/Gas4.

2 On a plate, mix together the pistachios, sesame seeds, parsley, lemon zest, onion powder, chilli powder, cumin and coriander. Season with salt and pepper.

3 Dunk each of the chicken breasts into the mixture and press down on each side to coat thoroughly.

4 Heat the oil in an oven-safe pan and sear the chicken breasts for 1-2 minutes on each side, until the crust turns golden.

5 Arrange the lemon slices around the chicken, cover the pan, and bake in the oven for 25 minutes. Remove the cover and bake for another 5 minutes or so, until the chicken crust is crispy.

6 Serve the chicken breasts with some juices from the pan.

Chefs Note....
Make a non-spicy version by reducing or omitting the chilli, cumin and coriander. Just increase the quantities of the other crust ingredients instead.

Turkey and Cheese Burgers

KETO DIET
FOR BEGINNERS

Ingredients

- 4 tbsp cream cheese
- 50g/2oz Cheddar cheese, grated
- ¼ tsp garlic granules
- 1 fresh chilli, deseeded & finely chopped

- ½ onion, peeled & finely chopped
- 750g/1lb11oz lean turkey, minced
- Salt & pepper
- 1 tbsp olive oil

Method

1 Preheat the grill and line the grill pan with foil.

2 In a small bowl, mix together the cream cheese, Cheddar, garlic granules and chilli.

3 In a larger bowl, mix the onion into the turkey and season well with salt and pepper. Shape it with your hands and divide it evenly into 4 pieces.

4 Take about a quarter of the cheese mixture and shape it into a small pancake. Fold one of the turkey pieces around it and form it into a burger shape. Repeat until you have 4 burgers. Brush each of them all over with olive oil and place them in the grill pan.

5 Grill the burgers for about 6 minutes on each side, or until they're completely cooked.

6 Serve with crunchy green salad and tomatoes, and guacamole or tomato sauce.

Chefs Note....
A great way to use up leftover Christmas turkey!

Pork Chops in Gravy

KETO DIET
FOR BEGINNERS

Ingredients

- 1 tbsp paprika
- 1 tsp garlic granules
- 1 tsp dried onion granules
- 4 boneless pork chops, each weighing approx. 150g/5oz
- 1 tsp black pepper
- 1 tsp salt
- ¼ tsp Cayenne pepper

- 2 tbsp coconut oil
- ½ onion, peeled & sliced
- 175g/6oz mushrooms, sliced
- 15g/½oz butter
- 120ml/½ cup double cream
- ¼ tsp xanthan gum
- 1 tbsp fresh parsley, chopped

Method

1 In a small bowl, mix together the paprika, garlic and onion granules, black pepper, salt, and Cayenne pepper. Use about 1 tbsp of the mix to rub evenly into the pork chops on both sides. Set the rest aside.

2 Melt the coconut oil in the frying pan and brown the pork chops for about 3 minutes on each side. Tip in the onion and mushrooms, reduce the heat, cover and cook for about 10 minutes.

3 With a slotted spoon, transfer the chops to a serving plate and keep warm.

4 Whisk the remaining spice mixture into the hot liquid in the pan, then stir in the butter, and the cream. Whisk in the xanthan gum and simmer for about 3 minutes until the butter is melted and the sauce begins to thicken. Remove from the heat.

5 Pour the gravy over the pork chops. Scatter parsley over the top, and serve.

Chefs Note....
Enjoy with cauliflower and broccoli.

Chicken and Broccoli Casserole

Ingredients

- 550g/1¼lb chicken breast, cooked and chopped into bite-sized pieces
- 2 tbsp olive oil
- 350g/12oz frozen broccoli
- 120ml/½ cup soured cream
- 120ml/½ cup double cream
- 100g/3½oz Cheddar cheese
- 3 rashers bacon, fried & crumbled
- Salt & pepper
- ½ tsp paprika
- 1 tsp dried oregano

Method

1 Preheat your oven to 200C/400F/Gas6. Grease a casserole dish.

2 In a large bowl, mix together the chicken, broccoli, olive oil and soured cream.

3 Turn it out into the casserole dish and spread into an even, compact layer.

4 Pour the double cream evenly over the top. Sprinkle on the paprika and oregano and season with salt and pepper.

5 Scatter the cheese evenly over the top and sprinkle with the bacon crumbs.

6 Bake the casserole in the oven for 20-25 minutes until it's bubbling and the edges are brown.

7 Serve hot.

Chefs Note....
Broccoli is a great source of dietary fibre, vitamins, calcium and omega 3.

Keto Chilli

Ingredients

- 900g/2lb minced beef
- 1 onion, peeled & chopped
- 1 red pepper, deseeded & chopped
- 1lt/4 cups tomato juice
- 2 x 400g/14oz tinned chopped tomatoes

- 425g/15oz tinned pumpkin puree
- 1 tbsp mixed spice
- 1 tbsp chilli powder
- 2 tsp Cayenne pepper
- 2 tsp ground cumin

Method

1 In a large pan, brown the mince. Strain it and return it to the pan. Tip in the onion and red pepper and cook for about 5 minutes until the onion is translucent.

2 Pour in the tomato juice, chopped tomatoes and pumpkin puree. Stir in the mixed spice, chilli powder, Cayenne pepper and cumin. Reduce the heat and simmer for half an hour.

3 Adjust the seasoning, then cook for another 30 minutes.

4 Serve with riced cauliflower.

Chefs Note....
To make cooked cauliflower 'rice' whizz the cauliflower in a food processor and microwave for a minute or two.

Mushroom Risotto

KETO DIET
FOR BEGINNERS

Ingredients

- 25g/1oz butter
- 2 tbsp olive oil
- 6 cloves garlic, peeled & crushed
- 1 onion, peeled & chopped
- 1 shallot, peeled & finely chopped
- 225g/8oz mushrooms, finely sliced

- 500ml/2 cups chicken stock, divided
- 450g/1lb riced cauliflower
- 250ml/1 cup double cream
- 50g/2oz Parmesan cheese, grated
- 2 tbsp fresh parsley
- Salt & pepper

Method

1 Heat the butter and oil in a large frying pan, and sauté the garlic, onion, and shallot for about 5 minutes until the onions are translucent.

2 Stir in the mushrooms and about half of the chicken stock.

3 Cook for another 5 minutes, until the mushrooms soften. Add the cauliflower rice and pour in the rest of the stock. Cook for 10 minutes, stirring frequently.

4 Lower the heat and stir in the cream, Parmesan and parsley.

5 Season with salt and pepper, and simmer for 10-15 minutes until the sauce thickens.

Chefs Note....
Feel free to add a glug or two of white wine with the stock.

Marinated Prawns with Sprouts

Ingredients

- 60ml/¼ cup soy sauce
- 2 tbsp rice vinegar
- 2 tbsp liquid sweetener
- 2 tsp agave nectar
- 1 tbsp sesame oil
- 1 clove garlic, peeled & crushed

- 450g/1lb large peeled prawns
- Cooking spray
- 450g/1lb Brussels sprouts, halved
- 2 tbsp olive oil
- Salt & pepper

Method

1. In a bowl combine the soy sauce, rice vinegar, sweetener, agave, sesame oil, and garlic. Pour half into another bowl or a plastic zip bag and marinate the shrimp in the liquid.

2. Preheat the oven to 200C/400F/Gas6. Grease a baking tray with non-stick spray.

3. In a bowl, toss the sprouts with the olive oil, and season them with salt and pepper. Arrange them on the baking tray and roast them in the oven for about 15 minutes.

4. Drain the prawns in a colander, and place them on the baking tray with the roasted sprouts. If necessary, move the sprouts out of the way so that the shrimp are in a single layer. Return the tray to the oven for 5 or 6 minutes or until the shrimp turn pink.

5. Stir the shrimp and sprouts together and brush them with the rest of the soy sauce marinade.

6. Serve at once.

Chefs Note....
Be careful not to overcook the prawns. If they're smaller, they'll need less time in the oven.

French Onion Soup

KETO DIET
FOR BEGINNERS

Ingredients

- 4 tbsp ghee
- 4 large onions, peeled & finely sliced
- 4 cloves garlic, peeled & finely chopped
- 1lt/4 cups chicken stock
- Salt & pepper
- 50g/2oz Gruyere cheese, grated

Method

1 Melt the ghee in a large pan, and sauté the onions until soft and beginning to caramelize.

2 Add the garlic, then pour in the stock. Season with salt and pepper and bring to the boil, stirring occasionally. Lower the heat and simmer for half an hour.

3 Ladle into bowls and serve sprinkled with the cheese.

Chefs Note....
Onions are great antioxidants and make delicious soup. Enjoy as part of your main meal or as lunch.

Noodles alla Carbonara

Ingredients

- 5g/1oz butter
- 4 rashers bacon
- 225g/8oz shirataki noodles
- 4 eggs

- 100g/3½oz Parmesan cheese, grated
- 2 cioves garlic, peeled & crushed
- Salt & pepper
- Parsley, to garnish

Method

1 Melt the butter in a large pan and fry the bacon until crisp.

2 Add the garlic and the noodles, then reduce the heat and cook, stirring frequently.

3 Meanwhile, whisk the eggs in a bowl with about 75g/3oz of the cheese.

4 When the noodles are hot, tip them into a separate bowl and, stirring constantly, pour in the egg mixture. Season to taste with salt and pepper.

5 Serve at once, sprinkled with parsley and the remaining Parmesan.

Chefs Note....
Shirataki noodles are made from the konjac yam and are the best keto substitute for spaghetti.

Sausage Casserole

KETO DIET FOR BEGINNERS

Ingredients

- 3 sausages
- 1 onion, peeled & sliced
- 125g/4oz mushrooms
- Salt & pepper
- ½ tsp dried oregano
- ½ tsp dried basil

- 125g/4oz passata
- 60ml/¼ cup red wine
- 1 tbsp mascarpone cheese
- 25g/1oz Parmesan cheese, grated
- 40g/1oz mozzarella cheese, grated

Method

1 Preheat your oven to 175C/350F/Gas4.

2 Fry the sausages in an ovenproof pan until they're mostly cooked. Remove them from the pan and sauté the onions and mushrooms.

3 Slice the sausages and return them to the pan. Season with salt and pepper, oregano and basil. Stir in the passata, wine, mascarpone and Parmesan.

4 Slide the pan into the oven and bake for about 15 minutes. Scatter the mozzarella over the top and bake for another couple of minutes.

5 Serve and enjoy!

Chefs Note....
Use your favourite everyday sausages or go for Italian sausages or chorizo for a change.

KETO DIET
DESSERTS

LOSE WEIGHT FOR GOOD
THE KETO DIET FOR BEGINNERS

Tiramisu

KETO DIET
FOR BEGINNERS

Ingredients

- 5 eggs, separated, + 5 more, separated in different bowls
- Salt
- 50g/2oz no-carb natural sweetener, + 125g/4oz, + 75g/3oz
- 75g/3oz coconut flour
- 50g/2oz whey protein powder
- Zest of 1 lemon
- 300g/11oz mascarpone cheese
- 1 cup of strong brewed coffee
- 60ml/¼ cup marsala wine
- Cocoa powder for dusting

Method

1 Preheat the oven to 190C/375F/Gas5. Line a baking tray with parchment. With an electric mixer, whisk 5 of the egg whites with a pinch of salt. When they're foamy, add about 50g/2oz of the sweetener and whisk them into stiff peaks.

2 In a bowl whisk the egg yolks with 125g/4oz sweetener and the lemon zest, until the sweetener dissolves. Gently fold the egg whites into the yolks.

3 In a small bowl, mix together the coconut flour and the whey protein. Sieve it into the egg mix and gently stir to mix thoroughly into a light, fluffy dough. Spoon the dough onto the baking tray, making "sponge finger" shapes. Bake for 15 minutes until golden. Allow them to cool completely.

4 In a clean bowl, whisk 5 egg whites with a pinch of salt.

5 In another bowl, whisk the yolks with 75g/3oz sweetener until the sweeter dissolves. Whisk in the mascarpone until the mixture is well blended, then fold in the egg whites.

6 In a small bowl, mix together the coffee and the marsala. Dip the cooled sponge fingers into the coffee.

7 Take 6 serving glasses and place the coffee-soaked sponge fingers at the bottom of each. Spoon mascarpone over the top, then add the cream and dust with cocoa powder. Repeat the layers until you've used everything up. Chill in the fridge for 2 hours or so, and then serve.

Chocolate Chip Ice Cream

Ingredients

- 250ml/1 cup double cream
- 125g/4oz cup powdered sweetener
- 175g/6oz ricotta cheese

- 75g/3oz cream cheese, room temperature
- 1 tsp vanilla extract
- 60g/2½oz sugar-free chocolate chips

Method

1 Whisk the cream in a bowl with half the sweetener until it forms stiff peaks.

2 In a blender or food processor, blend together the ricotta, cream cheese, vanilla, and the remaining sweetener. When it's smooth, fold it into the whipped cream. Fold the chocolate chips into the mixture.

3 Turn the mixture out into an airtight container and freeze for at least 6 hours until the ice cream is firm.

4 Serve alone or sprinkled with a few fresh berries or chopped nuts.

Chefs Note....
If the ice cream has been frozen for longer than 6 hours, you might need to thaw it a little before you serve.

Lemon Meringue Pie

Ingredients

- 3 tbsp coconut oil
- 60g/2½oz gluten free flour
- 120ml/½ cup maple syrup, + 1 tbsp
- 250ml/1 cup water

- 6 eggs, separated
- 2 lemons, zested and juiced, + a few drops more
- 1 gluten-free pastry base, baked
- 1 tsp vanilla extract

Method

1 Melt the coconut oil in a pan. Stir in the flour to create a roux. Gradually stir in 120ml/½ cup maple syrup and the water until the mixture thickens, then lower the heat.

2 Whisk the eggs yolks in a small bowl. Stirring constantly, pour in about a quarter of the sauce, then pour all the egg mixture into the pan with the sauce, stirring.

3 Stir in the lemon juice and lemon zest until it forms a lemon curd-like mixture. Pour it into the pastry base and leave to cool.

4 Chill it in the fridge for a couple of hours.

5 Preheat the oven to 200C/400F/Gas6.

6 Whisk the egg whites in a bowl with a few drops of lemon juice for about 10 minutes. Then whisk in 1 tbsp maple syrup and the vanilla until it forms peaks.

7 Spread the meringue on top of the chilled pie, creating peaks as you go. Bake in the oven for about 8 minutes, or until the meringue is as brown as you like it.

8 Slice and serve.

Chefs Note....
Buy a suitable ready-made pie base, or bake your own in advance.

Coconut Cream Pies

Ingredients

- 50g/2oz butter
- 50g/2oz sweetener, + 50g/2oz, + 2 tbsp
- 50g/2oz almond flour
- 25g/1oz coconut flakes, + 2 tbsp
- 250ml/1 cup double cream, 60ml/¼ cup

- 2 egg yolks
- 25g/1oz coconut flour
- 120ml/½ cup water
- 1 tsp vanilla extract, + 1 tsp

Method

1 Gently melt the butter in a pan. Stir in 50g/2oz sweetener until it dissolves, then stir in the almond flour and coconut flakes.

2 Divide the mixture between 4 ramekins and flatten it down with the back of your spoon. Allow to cool.

3 Meanwhile, in a fresh pan, gently heat 250ml/1 cup cream. In a bowl, whisk the egg yolks with the coconut flour and water.

4 Stir 1 tsp vanilla and 50g/2oz sweetener into the cream in the pan, then whisk in the egg and flour mixture until it thickens.

5 Leave it to cool for about 5 minutes, then spoon it over the crust in the ramekins. Chill in the ridge for at least an hour.

6 Gently toast the remaining 2 tbsp coconut flakes, stirring frequently until they're golden brown.

7 In a large bowl, whisk the remaining 60ml/¼ cup cream with 1 tsp vanilla and 2 tbsp sweetener, until it forms peaks.

8 When you're ready to eat, spoon the cream on top of the custard in the ramekins, and scatter the coconut flakes on top.

9 Serve and enjoy!

Chefs Note....
Coconut flour makes a good thickener for the custard, but if you can't get it, use a pinch of xanthan gum instead.

Berry Crumble

Ingredients

- 1 tbsp coconut oil
- 300g/11oz mix of raspberries, strawberries, blueberries etc.
- 140g/4½oz almonds
- 50g/2oz pecan nuts

- 25g/1oz butter
- 1 tsp cinnamon
- 1 tsp vanilla extract
- ¼ tsp sea salt

Method

1 Preheat the grill.

2 Heat the coconut oil in a large frying pan and cook the berries in it for about 4 minutes until they soften.

3 Tip the nuts into your food processor. Add the butter, cinnamon, vanilla extract and salt. Pulse for a few seconds to make a crumble.

4 Scatter the nut mixture over the fruit and slide under the grill for 8 minutes or so, until the crumble is golden brown and crisp.

5 Serve warm or cold as you prefer, with cream or yogurt if you wish.

Chefs Note....
If you have a sweeter tooth, you might like to add a few drops of liquid sweetener to the fruit as it's cooking, and to the crumble.

Chia and Coconut Brownies

Ingredients

- 100g/3½oz desiccated coconut
- 4 tbsp chia seeds
- 500ml/2 cups water
- 1 egg

- 125g/4oz unsweetened cooking chocolate
- 2 tbsp coconut oil
- 2 tbsp sweetener
- 125g/4oz fresh raspberries

Method

1 Preheat the oven to 175C/350F/Gas4. Grease a baking dish.

2 Soak the chia seeds in 250ml/1 cup water.

3 In a different bowl soak the coconut in another 250ml/1 cup water. Soak them both for about 10 minutes, then blend them with the egg to make a smooth cream.

4 Gently melt the cooking chocolate in a pan with the coconut oil and the sweetener. Scrape it all into the blender with the chia and coconut mixture.

5 Blend them together then pour the mixture into the baking dish.

6 Scatter on the raspberries, mixing some in and leaving the rest on top. Bake in the oven for about half an hour until the cake is firm at the edges but still soft in the centre.

7 Allow to cool for a few minutes before serving with cream or keto-friendly ice cream.

Chefs Note....
Chia seeds and coconut are both rich in dietary fibre, so these brownies are both delicious and good for you!

Simple Strawberry Cakes

KETO DIET
FOR BEGINNERS

Ingredients

- 25g/1oz butter, melted
- 2 tbsp sweetener, + 1 tbsp for the cream
- 25g/1oz almond flour
- 1 tbsp coconut flour
- 1 egg
- ½ tsp baking powder

- 60g/2½oz pureed strawberries, + 2 tbsp for the cream
- pinch of salt
- ½tsp vanilla extract
- 120ml/½ cup double cream

Method

1 In a bowl, stir the melted butter together with the sweetener, almond and coconut flours, the egg, 60g/2½oz strawberry puree, baking powder, salt and vanilla.

2 Divide this batter between 2 mugs, and microwave them for 90 seconds.

3 Insert a cocktail stick and if it doesn't come out clean, microwave for a few seconds more, until it does.

4 Allow the cakes to cool.

5 Meanwhile, whisk the cream in a bowl until it forms stiff peaks. In a separate bowl, mix the strawberry puree and the sweetener.

6 Fold the strawberry gently into the whipped cream and dollop or pipe it onto the cakes.

Chefs Note....
Alternatively, you can bake the cakes in 4 baking paper cups in the oven at 190C/375F/Gas5 for 20 minutes.

Lemon and Strawberry Pie

KETO DIET FOR BEGINNERS

Ingredients

- 150g/5oz almond flour
- 50g/2oz sweetener, + 125g/4oz
- ¼ tsp salt
- 50g/2oz butter, melted
- 160g/5oz strawberries, chopped

- ½ tsp lemon extract
- Juice of 2 lemons, + zest of 1
- 4 egg yolks, + 1 egg
- 250ml/1 cup double cream

Method

1 In a bowl, mix the almond flour with 50g/2oz sweetener, and salt. Stir in the melted butter.

2 Scrape the mixture out into a pie dish and spread it evenly, pressing it firmly into the bottom and sides. Place the dish in the freezer to chill quickly.

3 Meanwhile, blend together the strawberries, 125g/4oz sweetener, the lemon extract and lemon juice, until smooth.

4 Set a bowl over a pan of simmering water. In the bowl, combine the egg yolks and the whole egg. Whisk for about 8 minutes until they thicken.

5 Remove the bowl from the heat and whisk in the strawberry and lemon puree. Allow to cool to room temperature.

6 In another bowl, whip the cream until it forms stiff peaks, then gently fold in the egg and strawberry mixture and the lemon zest.

7 Spread the filling inside the chilled crust and return it to the freezer for at least 6 hours, until the filling is set and firm.

8 Slice and serve.

Chefs Note....
Use organic cream if you can. It has no starches or thickeners and therefore it has less carbs.

Chocolate Soufflés

KETO DIET
FOR BEGINNERS

Ingredients

- Butter for greasing, + 60g/2½oz
- Coconut sugar for dusting, + 50g/2oz
- 150g/5oz dark chocolate
- 3 tsp orange zest
- 1 tsp vanilla extract

- 3 tbsp almond flour
- 1 tbsp arrowroot starch
- 250ml/1 cup coconut milk
- 2 egg yolks, + 4 egg whites
- ½ tsp lemon juice

Method

1 Preheat the oven to 175C/350F/Gas4.

2 Grease 6 ramekins with a little butter. Dust them lightly with coconut sugar.

3 Melt the chocolate and stir in the orange zest and vanilla extract.

4 Melt 60g/2½oz butter in a separate pan. Whisk in the almond flour and arrowroot starch to make a roux, and gradually whisk in the milk until you have a thick sauce. Stir in the chocolate mixture until thoroughly blended. Then, stir in the egg yolks.

5 Beat the egg whites in a bowl with the lemon juice.

Gradually whisk in the sugar until you have foamy peaks.

6 Pour the chocolate mixture into a large bowl, and gently fold in the egg whites, about a third at a time.

7 Pour the mixture into the ramekins, leaving about a cm at the top. Bake in the oven for 20-25 minutes until the soufflés rise. Sprinkle them with coconut sugar and serve at once.

Chefs Note....
Use dark chocolate that has at least 75 % cocoa.

Peanut Butter Balls

KETO DIET
FOR BEGINNERS

Ingredients

- 3 tbsp smooth peanut butter
- 3 tsp unsweetened cocoa powder
- 2½ tsp powdered sweetener

- 2 tsp almond flour
- 40g/1½oz coconut flakes

Method

1 In a bowl, combine the peanut butter with the cocoa, sweetener and flour.

2 Place it in the freezer for an hour.

3 Then, tip the coconut flakes onto a plate or board. With a melon baller, scoop out a peanut butter ball and drop it in the coconut. Roll it around to coat thoroughly. Repeat with the rest of the peanut butter.

4 Chill the coated balls in the fridge for a few hours, or preferably overnight, to firm them up.

5 Serve and enjoy!

Chefs Note....

If you're in a hurry, you can omit freezing the peanut butter mix before making the balls, but it will be messier and the balls more difficult to work with.

Chocolate and Nut Bark

Ingredients

- 75g/3oz almonds
- 40g/1½oz coconut flakes
- 100g/3½oz dark chocolate

- 125g/4oz coconut butter
- ½ tsp almond extract
- ¼ tsp sea salt

Method

1 Preheat the oven to 175C/350F/Gas4. Line one baking tray with foil, and another with parchment.

2 Arrange the almonds and coconut flakes on the foil-lined baking tray and toast in the oven for about 7 minutes, shaking once during cooking. Set aside to cool.

3 Melt the chocolate in the microwave, a few seconds at a time, then stir in the coconut butter and the almond extract.

4 Pour the mixture onto the parchment lined baking tray and spread it out evenly. Scatter the toasted almonds and coconut flakes over the top.

5 Sprinkle with sea salt, and chill in the fridge for at least an hour until the chocolate has set and hardened.

6 Break it up or slice it to serve.

Chefs Note....
Feel free to add a few drops of liquid sweetener to the melted chocolate.

Coffee Custard

Ingredients

- 50g/2oz butter
- 125g/4oz mascarpone cheese
- 2 tsp instant coffee powder

- 4 eggs, separated
- 1 tsp liquid sweetener
- ¼ tsp cream of tartar

Method

1 Melt the butter and the mascarpone together in a pan, then whisk in the coffee and the egg yolks.

2 Cook gently, stirring occasionally, until the mixture thickens.

3 Take the pan off the heat and stir in the sweetener.

4 In a bowl, whisk together the egg whites and cream of tartar, until they form stiff peaks. Gently fold this into the mixture in the pan.

5 Pour into individual glasses and chill in the fridge for an hour or so before serving.

Chefs Note....
Feel free to use any liquid sweetener, or combination of sweeteners, that you like.

Peanut Butter Mousse

SERVES 3

KETO DIET
FOR BEGINNERS

Ingredients

- 1 tsp gelatine
- 1 tbsp cold water
- 1½ tbsp boiling water

- 250ml/1 cup double cream
- 225g/8oz smooth peanut butter
- 75g/3oz powdered sweetener

Method

1 Sprinkle the gelatine over the cold water in a small bowl and leave for 2 minutes, then stir in the boiling water until the gelatine is dissolved.

2 In a larger bowl, whip the cream until thick. In a separate bowl, whisk together the peanut butter, and sweetener.

3 Gently fold the cream into the peanut butter, then stir in the gelatine.

4 Using an electric mixer, whisk the mixture until it's fluffy.

5 Divide the mixture between dessert bowls, and enjoy!

Chefs Note....
If you like, top with a few whole hazel nuts or dark chocolate chips.

Lemon Mousse

KETO DIET
FOR BEGINNERS

Ingredients

- 225g/8oz mascarpone cheese
- 2 lemons, juiced, + ½ tsp zest
- 250ml/1 cup double cream

- 1 tsp liquid sweetener
- Pinch salt

Method

1 In your blender or food processer, blend together the mascarpone and lemon juice. When it's smooth, blend in the cream, sweetener and lemon zest.

2 Divide into glasses and chill in the fridge for an hour or so before serving.

3 Sprinkle with additional lemon zest if you wish.

Chefs Note....
A delicious creamy dessert you will enjoy on its own. You can also use it on a cheesecake base.

Vanilla Fat Bombs

Ingredients

- 4 tbsp coconut oil
- 25g/1oz cacao butter, or cocoa butter
- 10 drops vanilla stevia

Method

1 In a pan, gently melt together the coconut oil and the cacao butter.

2 When they're melted and blended together, take the pan off the heat and stir in the vanilla stevia.

3 Pour the mixture into small tart moulds and chill them in the fridge until they've hardened.

4 Serve, or keep in the fridge until needed.

Chefs Note....
As well as making a buttery, chocolatey dessert or snack, this is a great way to boost your energy levels through fat.

KETO DIET
DRINKS

LOSE
WEIGHT
FOR GOOD
THE KETO DIET
FOR BEGINNERS

Raspberry and Cream Cheese Smoothie

KETO DIET
FOR BEGINNERS

Ingredients

- 60g/2½oz raspberries
- 25g/1oz cream cheese
- 250ml/1 cup almond milk
- 1 tbsp sugar-free vanilla syrup

Method

1 Tip the raspberries into your blender.

2 Add the cream cheese then pour in the almond milk and the syrup.

3 Blend until smooth.

4 Pour into a glass and enjoy!

Chefs Note....
A delicious and filling smoothie with less than 4 carbs. Use either fresh or frozen raspberries, and if you can't get vanilla syrup from your local shop, it's available from online retailers.

Rhubarb and Strawberry Smoothie

KETO DIET FOR BEGINNERS

Ingredients

- 50g/2oz rhubarb, roughly chopped
- 40g/1½oz strawberries
- 25g/1oz almonds
- 1 tsp freshly grated ginger
- 1 egg

- 120ml/½ cup unsweetened almond milk
- 2 tbsp double cream
- ½ tsp vanilla extract
- 5 drops liquid sweetener

Method

1 Tip the strawberries, rhubarb and almonds into your blender.

2 Add the ginger and the egg, then pour in the almond milk, cream, vanilla extract and sweetener.

3 Blend until smooth.

4 Pour into a glass and serve.

Chefs Note....
Use almond butter instead of almonds if you prefer.

Avocado and Almond Smoothie

KETO DIET
FOR BEGINNERS

Ingredients

- 1 tbsp chia seeds
- 3 tbsp water
- ½ avocado, stoned, frozen
- 1 tbsp almond butter

- 2 tsp cocoa powder
- 250ml/1 cup unsweetened almond milk
- 1 tbsp coconut oil, melted
- A few ice cubes

Method

1 Soak the chia seeds in the water for 10 minutes, then tip them into your blender.

2 Add the avocado, almond butter and cocoa.

3 Pour in the almond milk and coconut oil.

4 Add a few ice cubes, if you wish.

5 Blend until smooth, then pour into a glass and serve.

Chefs Note....
High fat, high protein, low carb – and delicious! Feel free to substitute the nut milk and butter – e.g. try with coconut instead of almond.

Green Detox Smoothie

KETO DIET
FOR BEGINNERS

Ingredients

- 40g/2½oz lettuce
- 25g/1oz blackberries
- 75g/3oz cucumber, chopped
- 1 kiwi fruit, peeled and chopped
- 1 tbsp fresh parsley

- ½ avocado, stoned. peeled & roughly chopped
- 2 tsp freshly grated ginger,
- 1 tbsp sweetener
- 500ml/2 cups coconut milk

Method

1 Drop the lettuce, blackberries, cucumber, kiwi and avocado into your blender.

2 Add the parsley, ginger and sweetener and pour in the water.

3 Blend until smooth.

4 Pour into 2 or 3 glasses and serve.

Chefs Note....
A great detox, low carb smoothie to start your day.

SERVES 2

Raspberry and Nut Smoothie

KETO DIET
FOR BEGINNERS

Ingredients

- 125g/4oz raspberries
- 50g/2oz almond flour
- 2 tbsp peanut butter
- 225g/8oz Greek yogurt

- 125ml/½ cup unsweetened almond milk
- 1 tsp sweetener
- 4 ice cubes

Method

1 Tip the raspberries and flour into your blender.

2 Add the peanut butter and yogurt and then pour in the almond milk. Add the sweetener.

3 Blend until smooth.

4 Add the ice and blend again until completely smooth.

5 Pour into 2 glasses and serve immediately.

Chefs Note....
Omit the ice if your blender can't handle it – the smoothie will still taste great.

Strawberry Mint Smoothie

KETO DIET FOR BEGINNERS

Ingredients

- 5 frozen strawberries
- Fresh mint leaves
- 2 tbsp double cream

- 250ml/1 cup coconut milk
- 1 tbsp sugar-free vanilla syrup

Method

1 Tip the strawberries into your blender with the mint.

2 Pour in the cream, coconut milk and syrup.

3 Blend until smooth.

4 Pour into a glass and enjoy!

Chefs Note....
Try with almond milk or cow's milk if you prefer.

Matcha Milk

KETO DIET
FOR BEGINNERS

Ingredients

- 250ml/1 cup unsweetened cashew milk
- 1 tbsp coconut oil, melted
- 1 tsp matcha powder
- ¼ tsp vanilla seeds (or vanilla extract)
- 2 ice cubes
- Sprinkling cocoa powder

Method

1 Pour the cashew milk into your blender with the coconut oil.

2 Add the matcha powder and vanilla, then drop in a couple of ice cubes.

3 Blend until the drink is the consistency you want.

4 Pour it into a glass and sprinkle a little cocoa powder on top.

5 Drink!

Chefs Note....
Among other health benefits, matcha is rich in dietary fibre and antioxidants. It also helps boost the metabolism and burn calories.

Buttery Hot Chocolate

Ingredients

- 15g/½oz unsalted butter
- 2 tbsp cocoa powder
- ½ tsp vanilla extract

- 500ml/2 cups boiling water
- 2 tbsp double cream, whipped

Method

1 Divide the butter, cocoa and vanilla between 2 mugs.

2 Pour the boiling water into each and mix vigorously. Use a hand blender if you wish.

3 When the tops are foamy, add the cream. Enjoy!

Chefs Note....
You can use coconut cream instead, or leave the cream out altogether if you wish – it's still delicious keto goodness.